JAPAN

By Sloane Gould and
Joanne Mattern

EXPLORING WORLD CULTURES

Cavendish Square

Published in 2026 by Cavendish Square Publishing, LLC
2544 Clinton Street, Buffalo, NY 14224

Second Edition

Website: cavendishsq.com

Library of Congress Cataloging-in-Publication Data

Names: Gould, Sloane, author.
Title: Japan / Sloane Gould.
Description: Second edition. | New York : Cavendish Square Publishing, [2026] | Series: Exploring world cultures | "First edition by Joanne Mattern. Second edition by Sloane Gould." | Includes bibliographical references and index.
Identifiers: LCCN 2024040849 (print) | LCCN 2024040850 (ebook) | ISBN 9781502673480 (lib. bdg.) | ISBN 9781502673473 (paperback) | ISBN 9781502673497 (ebook)
Subjects: LCSH: Japan--Juvenile literature.
Classification: LCC DS806 .M384 2026 (print) | LCC DS806 (ebook) | DDC 952--dc23/eng/20241219
LC record available at https://lccn.loc.gov/2024040849
LC ebook record available at https://lccn.loc.gov/2024040850

Writers: Joanne Mattern; Sloane Gould (second edition)
Editor: Caitie McAneney
Copyeditor: Jill Keppeler
Designer: Deanna Lepovich

The photographs in this book are used by permission and through the courtesy of: Cover milatas/Shutterstock.com; p. 4 Guitar photographer/Shutterstock.com; p. 5 Giacomo Fatigati/Shutterstock.com; p. 6 Sarfaraz82/Shutterstock.com; p. 7 basiczto/Shutterstock.com; p. 8 Sean Pavone/Shutterstock.com; p. 9 Paolo Gallo/Shutterstock.com; p. 10 Savvapanf Photo/Shutterstock.com; p. 11 shutter_tonko/Shutterstock.com; p. 12 BoonritP/Shutterstock.com; p. 13 shisu_ka/Shutterstock.com; p. 15 (top) mapman/Shutterstock.com; p. 15 (bottom) GrooveZ/Shutterstock.com; p. 16 PixHound/Shuterstock.com; pp. 17, 19 PeopleImages.com - Yuri A/Shutterstock.com; p. 18 Steve Allen/Shutterstock.com; p. 20 Luciano Mortula - LGM/Shutterstock.com; p. 21 ESB Professional/Shutterstock.com; p. 22 ucchie79/Shutterstock.com; p. 23 Felix Lipov/Shutterstock.com; p. 24 Sergio Arjona/Shutterstock.com; p. 25 Tsunami by hokusai 19th century/Wikimedia Commons; p. 26 Anna Jurkovska/Shutterstock.com; p. 27 yu_photo/Shutterstock.com; p. 28 kattyart/Shutterstock.com; p. 29 oneinchpunch/Shutterstock.com.

CPSIA compliance information: Batch #CS26CSQ: For further information contact Cavendish Square Publishing LLC at 1-877-980-4450.

Printed in the United States of America

CONTENTS

INTRODUCTION

Japan is known as the "Land of the Rising Sun." From its place on the eastern coast of Asia, it's one of the first countries to see the sun each day. Japan is a country of islands, mountains, and **volcanoes**. It's a land of great natural beauty, which is celebrated in the Shinto religion, or belief system, based in Japan.

Millions of people live in the capital city of Tokyo, Japan.

Japan has a long history. Some say that humans settled in the area at least 30,000 years ago! It was ruled by empires for thousands of years. Today, the country still has an emperor, even though this is more of a **symbol** than a position of power.

With busy cities and beautiful gardens, Japan is a great place to visit and learn about. People here work very hard for their families and their jobs but also know how to have fun and celebrate nature. Let's read more about this exciting country!

Japanese gardens mix natural beauty with beautiful bridges, gates, and statues.

GEOGRAPHY

Japan's location in the Pacific Ocean has long affected the way people live there. Its islands also touch the Sea of Japan, the East China Sea, and the Sea of Okhotsk. You need to take a boat or airplane to get from Japan to any other country.

FACT!
Japan covers 145,883 square miles (377,835 sq km). That's smaller than the U.S. state of California.

Japan is made up of over 14,000 islands! Most of these islands are very small. No one lives on them. Most people live on the four largest islands: Honshu, Hokkaido, Kyushu, and Shikoku. Tokyo is on the largest island, Honshu.

This map of Japan shows its closest neighbors: Korea, China, and Russia.

The Japanese islands are part of the Ring of Fire. This area of the world has many active volcanoes. There are about 110 active volcanoes in Japan. Most of Japan is covered with mountains. The Japanese Alps are the highest mountain range. These mountains are on the island of Honshu. Many of Japan's mountains are covered with thick forests.

Mount Fuji is the tallest mountain and volcano in Japan.

IT'S TECTONIC!

The crust of Earth is made of giant slabs called tectonic plates. Japan is located where some tectonic plates meet. When they move, earthquakes happen!

HISTORY

Japan was the birthplace of the Jomon **culture**, which started around 12,000 years ago. Jomon people caught fish and hunted for food. Later, they became rice farmers. The Ainu people likely also arrived in Japan around 12,000 years ago from Siberia. The Yayoi people came to Honshu from China and Korea about 2,300 years ago.

FACT!

According to stories, Jimmu Tenno was the first emperor of Japan. He came to power in 660 BCE.

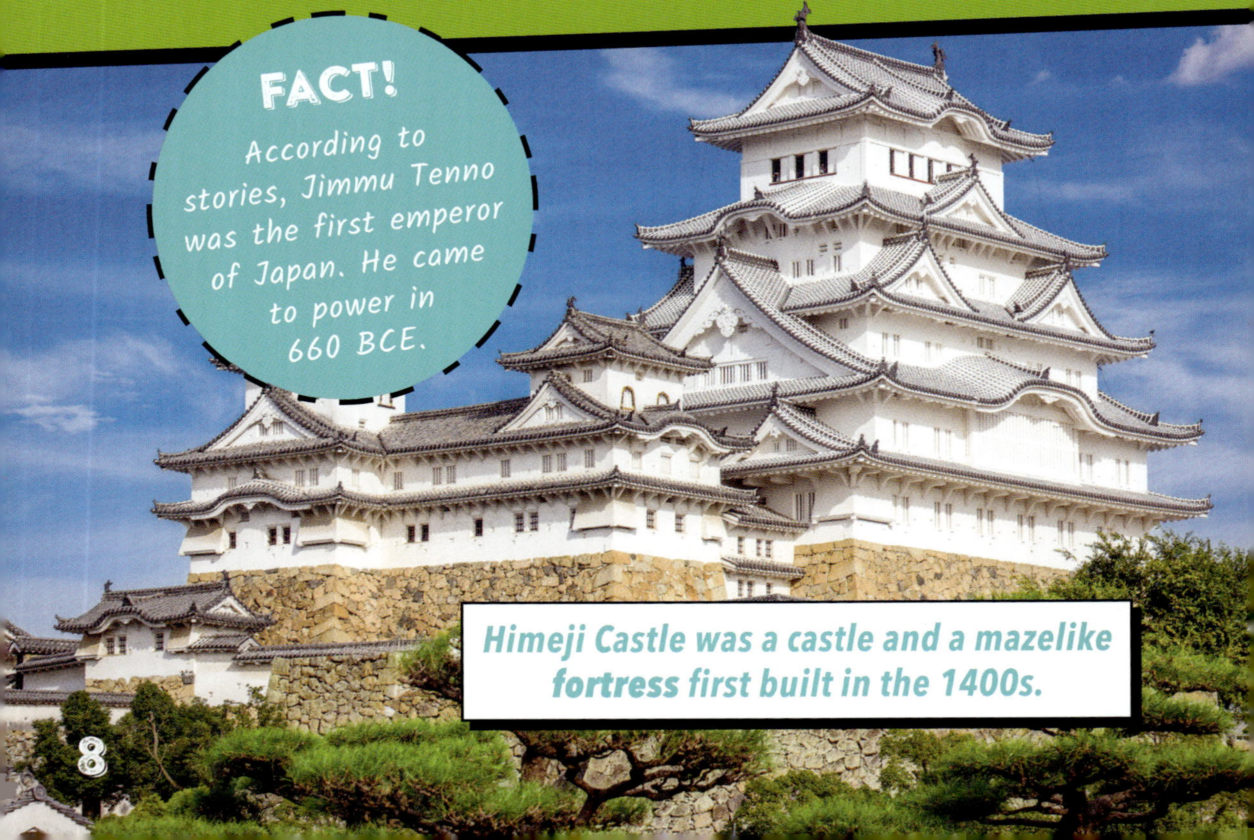

Himeji Castle was a castle and a mazelike fortress first built in the 1400s.

For a long time, emperors and shoguns ruled Japan. In early 1900s, Japan became very powerful. During World War II (1939-1945), Japan attacked a U.S. Navy base at Pearl Harbor in Hawaii. The United States then declared war on Japan. The war ended in 1945 after the United States dropped atomic bombs on two Japanese cities.

After the war, Japan changed. Public transportation improved, and people built factories to make different goods. Today, Japan has a strong **economy** and often works with the United States.

Japanese warriors were called samurai. This is samurai armor.

RULERS OF JAPAN

From around 660 BCE to the 1100s, Japan was ruled by emperors. After that, Japan was ruled by shoguns, or strong military leaders. Emperors ruled again starting in the 1800s.

GOVERNMENT

Japan is divided into 47 sections called prefectures. Japan still has an emperor, but this is mostly a **ceremonial** position. He does not have any real power. Instead, the Japanese government is led by a prime minister and a cabinet.

Japan's government is divided into three parts: executive, legislative, and judicial. The prime minister is the head of the executive branch. This branch carries out the laws. The prime minister is chosen by Japan's parliament. The parliament is Japan's legislative, or lawmaking, branch. It is called the Diet.

The Japanese flag is white with a red circle in the middle.

The judicial branch decides legal matters. The highest court is the Supreme Court. This court decides if cases follow the nation's constitution, or set of laws. After World War II, Japan wrote a new constitution modeled after the U.S. Constitution.

FACT!

Japan's government is a constitutional monarchy with a parliamentary government.

Japan's parliament meets in the National Diet Building in Tokyo.

THE DIET

The Diet has two houses. They are the House of Representatives and the House of Councillors. Japan's people vote for members of parliament.

THE ECONOMY

Japan's economy took off after World War II. Today, the country has one of the largest economies in the world. It's known as a major **technology** center. The nation makes cars, smartphones, cameras, computers, and more. Well-known Japanese brands include Sony, Toyota, and Canon. Robotics is a big **industry** in Japan. Some Japanese robots can talk and learn new tasks.

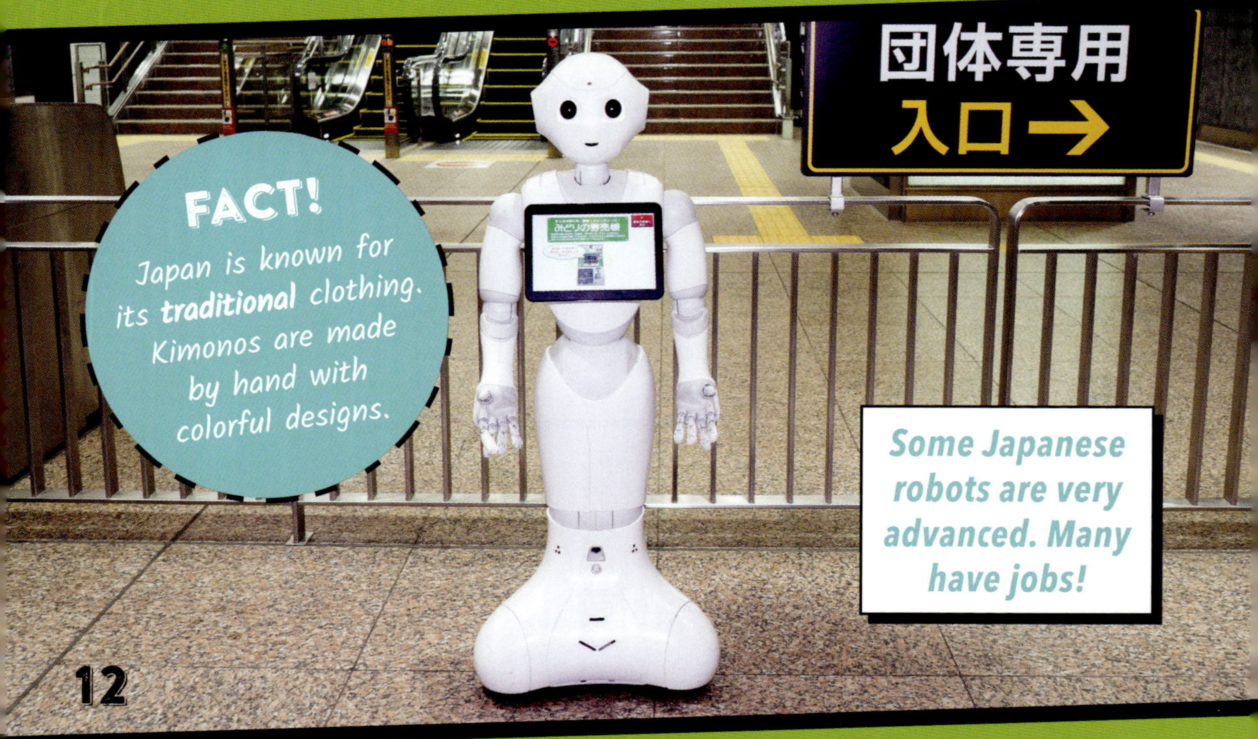

FACT!

*Japan is known for its **traditional** clothing. Kimonos are made by hand with colorful designs.*

Some Japanese robots are very advanced. Many have jobs!

About 70 percent of Japanese people work in the service industry. They work in stores, hotels, banks, and restaurants. They also work as teachers and lawyers and as bus and train drivers. People in Japan are known for working hard.

Agriculture is important in Japan. Farmers grow rice, potatoes, vegetables, apples, wheat, and tea. Fishing provides seafood like tuna, salmon, crabs, and shrimp. Fishing is an important industry in many coastal communities.

Japanese money is called yen.

TOURISM

Tourism is the business of people visiting a country. Tourism to Japan is a big industry. Millions of people visit Japan, especially Toyko, each year!

THE ENVIRONMENT

Japan's natural surroundings are unlike anywhere else in the world. It has many forests full of maples, cypresses, and beeches. Japan's most famous tree is the cherry tree.

Many animals live in Japan. Monkeys called macaques live on all the main islands except Hokkaido. Small animals in Japan include red foxes, sables, squirrels, and flying squirrels. Reptiles in Japan include many kinds of snakes and turtles. Beautiful Japanese birds include colorful pheasants and cranes. Giant salamanders live in some of Japan's rivers and streams.

With so many people, natural habitats can suffer. Many mammals in Japan, such as the Iriomote cat and the Tsushima leopard cat, are endangered, or at risk of dying out. In 2011, there was a huge earthquake and **tsunami** that caused a **nuclear** accident that harmed waters around Japan.

FACT!

Japan is home to Asiatic brown bears. They live everywhere, even near Japan's big cities!

Japanese macaques live the farthest north of all the monkeys in the world!

Cherry trees are one symbol of Japanese culture.

CHERRY BLOSSOMS

People come from around the world to see the beautiful pink cherry blossoms every spring in Japan. There are even festivals to celebrate these pretty trees.

THE PEOPLE TODAY

More than 123.2 million people live in Japan. People in Japan live longer than those almost anywhere else because of their healthy habits. The average Japanese person lives for more than 85 years.

Most Japanese people come from the ancient groups who lived during the Jomon and Yayoi periods. The Ainu people are also native to Japan. Today, the Ainu are a **minority** group with their own culture. The Ainu mostly live in northern Hokkaido.

The Ainu are Indigenous, or Native, people of northern Japan.

A small percent of the population comes from China or Korea. Others came from the Philippines, Indonesia, and Brazil. A minority group called the Ryukyuan people lives on the Ryukyu Islands. These islands didn't formally become part of Japan until 1879.

FACT!

More than 97 percent of people who live in Japan are ethnically Japanese.

People in Japan value the nation's rich culture.

ORIGINS OF THE AINU

Many thousands of years ago, Russia and Japan were closer together. Because of this, it is likely that the Ainu people came from Russia.

LIFESTYLE

Around 92 percent of Japan's population lives in cities. The most populated cities are Tokyo, Yokohama, Osaka, and Nagoya. Japanese cities are very crowded. People often live in apartments and get around by walking, biking, or taking public transportation. Japan has superfast rail travel on its world-famous bullet trains. Life is slower paced in the countryside, and fewer people live in these communities.

FACT!

Japanese men are expected to work hard to support their families. Around 75 percent of Japanese women also work.

The Japanese bullet train is called Shinkansen. It's a great way to get around Japan!

Bowing is the traditional way to greet someone in Japan.

Education is very important in Japan. Students start school when they are around six years old. The law says they must go to school for nine years. After that, almost all Japanese students go to high school. About half of them then go on to a university. Students must pass a difficult exam to get into a university. Many students go to special schools called cram schools for extra help. These extra classes can last five hours after the regular school day!

FAMILY TIME

Most Japanese families are small. They usually have one or two children. Family is very important to the Japanese people.

RELIGION

Shinto is a main religion in Japan, with more than 48 percent of people practicing it. Shinto began in Japan thousands of years ago. It says that there are many spirits called kami. Shinto rituals, or special actions, are done for good luck and positivity. Large Shinto shrines, or religious buildings, are found all over Japan.

SHINTO ARCHITECTURE

Shinto shrines are an important part of Japanese architecture, or buildings. You can see Shinto structures all over Japan, such as special torii gates.

This is a famous floating torii gate in Japan.

This is the Reclining Buddha of Nanzoin Temple.

FACT!
Buddhists believe that a person's soul can come back to live many different lives.

Buddhism is another ancient religion, with about 46 percent of Japanese people practicing. (Many practice it and Shinto.) Buddhism started in India, and Korean and Chinese immigrants brought it to Japan. Japan has several giant statues of Buddha, the main figure in Buddhism. One statue on the island of Kyushu is 134 feet (41 m) long. It's called the Reclining Buddha. That means he's resting!

Europeans brought Christianity to Japan hundreds of years ago. At one time, the government banned Christianity. Today, about 1 percent of the population is Christian.

LANGUAGE

Japanese is the main language in Japan. It's a hard language to learn! Japanese writing does not use letters. Instead, it uses symbols called characters. There are thousands of different Japanese characters! Calligraphy is the art of writing Japanese characters with a brush and ink. Children often learn this art in school.

OTHER LANGUAGES

The Ainu people have their own language. So do the people on the Ryukyu Islands. Hachijo is another ancient language spoken on a few small islands.

There are three different kinds of characters in Japan. They are called *kanji*, *hiragana*, and *katakana*. Kanji were taken from Chinese writing. Hiragana usually are used to help write native Japanese words. Katakana usually are used to spell words from other countries. A person may need to know over 3,000 characters just to read a Japanese newspaper!

FACT!

Katakana characters are used by most Japanese people for texting and emailing.

If you want to say hello in Japan, you can say *konnichiwa* (koh-NEE-chee-wah). To say thank you, you can say *arigatou* (ah-REE-gah-toh).

Many people visit Japan! Because of that, many signs show Japanese and English.

ARTS AND FESTIVALS

Japan is known around the world for its traditional and modern art. Origami is a traditional art. People fold paper to look like animals or other shapes. Modern Japanese art includes anime and manga. Manga are similar to comic books. People around the world enjoy anime, or Japanese animated movies and TV shows.

FACT!

Hayao Miyazaki is the most famous Japanese anime filmmaker.

Kintsugi is the Japanese art of repairing broken pottery with gold or another metal.

Japanese people celebrate many holidays and festivals, or special gatherings. They include traditional dances and music. Traditional musical instruments include drums and flutes. Rock and pop music are also popular in Japan.

Bon is a Buddhist festival that is held in the summer. During Bon, people remember those who have died. People light lanterns and send them out to sea. It's believed that spirits return to this world during this time.

One of the most famous paintings in Japan is **Under the Wave off Kanagawa** *by 19th-century artist Katsushika Hokusai.*

SHOGATSU

New Year's Day, or Shogatsu, is the biggest festival in Japan. It lasts for three days. People spend time with their family. They go to parades and eat special foods.

FUN AND PLAY

Japanese people work very hard, but they still know how to play and relax. Some people enjoy ikebana, or flower arranging. They set up beautiful flower arrangements. It is a relaxing hobby! Karate and judo are popular martial arts in Japan. Sumo wrestling is a traditional Japanese sport. This sport is more than 1,500 years old. Wrestlers push, pull, and slap each other.

FACT!

In sumo wrestling, each wrestler tries to push the other out of the ring or knock them down.

Judo began in the late 1800s in Japan.

Sports are very popular in Japan. Baseball is the most popular sport in the country. There are two different leagues, the Central League and the Pacific League. The Tokyo Giants are the most popular team. Several Japanese players have come to play in the United States. Some of the most famous Japanese baseball players include Ichiro Suzuki and Shohei Ohtani.

WINTER SPORTS

In northern Japan, where winters are cold and snowy, people enjoy skiing and snowboarding. You can ski in the Japanese Alps.

To see the Tokyo Giants play, you can go to the Tokyo Dome.

FOOD

Japanese food often is very healthy! People don't eat a lot of meat. Instead, they eat a lot of vegetables, rice, and fish. Sushi is a very popular Japanese dish. Sushi is made by wrapping rice and raw fish, vegetables, or other foods in seaweed. There are many kinds of sushi.

Sushi is eaten with chopsticks.

TASTY RAMEN

Ramen is a popular Japanese food. Ramen includes long noodles served in soup. The dish can include vegetables, eggs, and meat.

Japanese people also enjoy fruit and pickled vegetables. They eat many kinds of noodles. Soba noodles and udon noodles are very popular. So is a tasty noodle dish called ramen. Dumplings are also popular. They can be filled with meat, vegetables, or seafood.

Mochi is a popular dessert. Sticky rice is made into dough. Then the dough is stuffed with sweet bean paste or ice cream. The Japanese also enjoy pancakes and buns filled with sweet bean paste. It's common to drink tea with meals in Japan.

FACT!
Rice is the most common food in Japan. It is eaten at almost every meal.

Japanese tea ceremonies include preparing and drinking green tea in a special way.

GLOSSARY

ceremonial: Having to do with a ceremony, or special event that's been done for a long time.

culture: The beliefs and ways of life of a certain group of people.

economy: The amount of buying and selling in a place.

fortress: A structure built to keep people out or keep people safe.

industry: The businesses in an area.

minority: A group of people who are different from the larger group in a country or other area in some way.

nuclear: Having to do with the energy that's released when small parts of atoms, called nuclei, are split.

symbol: Something that stands for something else.

technology: A method that uses science to solve problems and the tools used to solve those problems.

traditional: Something that's been done for a long time.

tsunami: A huge sea wave caused by an earthquake.

volcano: An opening in Earth's crust through which liquid rock may flow.

FIND OUT MORE

Books

Doeden, Matt. *Travel to Japan*. Minneapolis, MN: Lerner Publications, 2022.

Hansen, Grace. *Himeji Castle*. Minneapolis, MN: Abdo Kids, 2022.

Kim, Cheryl. *Your Passport to Japan*. Oxford, UK: Raintree, 2024.

Websites

Japan
kids.britannica.com/kids/article/Japan/345715
Explore more fascinating facts about Japan's history and environment.

Japan Facts for Kids
www.kids-world-travel-guide.com/japan-facts.html
Discover more facts about Japan, written by kids for kids.

Video

Asia: Destination World
www.youtube.com/watch?v=nsOtOye-DJM
Travel to Asia with *National Geographic Kids*.

Publisher's note to educators and parents: Our editors have carefully reviewed these websites to ensure that they are suitable for students. Many websites change frequently, however, and we cannot guarantee that a site's future contents will continue to meet our high standards of quality and educational value. Be advised that students should be closely supervised whenever they access the internet.

INDEX